Start with Art

Drawing

Isabel Thomas

Heinemann Library
Chicago, Illinois

www.heinemannraintree.com
Visit our website to find out more information about Heinemann-Raintree books.

To order:
☎ Phone 888-454-2279
🖥 Visit www.heinemannraintree.com to browse our catalog and order online.

© 2012 Heinemann Library
an imprint of Capstone Global Library, LLC
Chicago, Illinois

Edited by Dan Nunn, Rebecca Rissman, and Catherine Veitch
Designed by Richard Parker
Picture research by Mica Brancic and Hannah Taylor
Originated by Capstone Global Library
Printed and bound in China by South China Printing
  Company Ltd

15 14 13 12 11
10 9 8 7 6 5 4 3 2 1

Library of Congress Cataloging-in-Publication Data
Thomas, Isabel, 1980-
  Drawing / Isabel Thomas.—1st ed.
    p. cm.—(Start with art)
  Includes bibliographical references and index.
  ISBN 978-1-4329-5016-3 (hardcover)—ISBN 978-1-4329-5023-1 (pbk.) 1. Drawing—Technique—Juvenile literature. I. Title.
  NC655.T427 2011
  741—dc22   2010042655

Acknowledgments
We would like to thank the following for permission to reproduce photographs: Alamy Images p. 4 (Cultura); © Capstone Publishers pp. 7, 8, 14, 20, 21, 22, 23 – tools (Karon Dubke), 15 (Erik Lervold); Corbis pp. 9 (Christie's Images), 11 (© Succession Picasso/DACS, London 2011); Rex Features p. 6 (Nils Jorgensen); Scala pp. 10, 13, 16 (© The Metropolitan Museum of Art/Art Resource New York); Shutterstock pp. 12 (© Studio 37), 17 (Václav Tauš), 23 – creative (© Monkey Business Images [Cultura]), 23 – gallery (© Shamleen), 23 – portrait (© Studio 37), 23 – self-portrait (© re_bekka), 23 – surface (©Evgenia Sh.), 23 – texture (© Konstantin Sutyagin); The Bridgeman Art Library pp. 5, 18 (Graphische Sammlung Albertina, Vienna, Austria), 19 (Private Collection/Photo © Lefevre Fine Art Ltd., London).

Front cover photograph of Self Portrait, 1912 (charcoal on paper) by Juan Gris (1887–1927), Lefevre Gallery reproduced with permission of The Bridgeman Art Library (Private Collection/Photo © Lefevre Fine Art Ltd., London). Back cover photograph of drawing tools reproduced with permission of © Capstone Publishers (Karon Dubke). Back cover photograph of portrait of a girl reproduced with permission of Shutterstock (© Studio 37).

Every effort has been made to contact copyright holders of material reproduced in this book. Any omissions will be rectified in subsequent printings if notice is given to the publisher.

Contents

Some words are shown in bold, **like this**. You can find out what they mean by looking in the glossary.

What Is a Drawing?

A drawing is a picture made up of
lines and other marks.

Artists make drawings to show what
they see or think.

This drawing of an elephant is 400 years old.

There were no cameras then. Drawings showed people what different animals looked like.

Where Can I See Drawings?

You can see drawings in a museum or **gallery**.

Many visitors come to look at drawings by famous artists.

Drawings are all around you, too.

Drawings in books show you what people in stories look like.

What Do People Use to Make Drawings?

People draw with all these **tools**.

They draw on flat **surfaces**, such as paper or cardboard.

Some Chinese artists draw with ink.

They use the ink to draw wide lines
and thin lines.

How Do People Make Drawings?

Drawings are made of different lines and shapes.

The straight lines, curved lines, and dots give this drawing **texture**.

This picture has long, curvy lines.

The artist added shapes and colors
to finish this picture of a dove.

Why Do People Make Drawings?

Drawings are a good way to show people your ideas.

You can draw things that you see, know, or remember.

Many artists draw things they see,
such as people, places, and objects.

Their drawings tell us about other
times and places.

What Else Do People Draw?

Some artists draw made-up things.

It is fun to be **creative**.

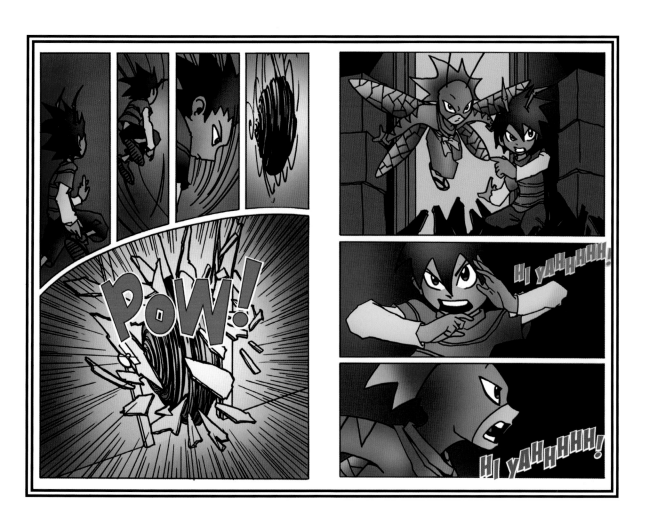

You can use drawings to tell a story.

A cartoon uses pictures instead
of words.

What Can Drawings Show?

Some artists make their drawings look real.

This **portrait** shows us what this shoemaker really looked like.

Drawings do not have to look real.

The shapes and lines in this drawing show a woman's face.

What Is a Self-Portrait?

If you cannot find anything to draw, try drawing yourself!

A famous artist drew this **self-portrait** when he was a boy.

Artists use self-portraits to tell us about themselves.

Do you think this artist was a happy or a grumpy person?

Start to Draw!

Some artists learn to draw by feeling things instead of looking at them.

1. Ask a friend to blindfold you.

2. Ask them to give you an object without telling you what it is.

3. Feel the object carefully, and then give it back to your friend.

4. Take your blindfold off and draw what you touched.

5. Make marks to show the shapes and **textures** that you felt.

6. Compare your drawing with the secret object!

Glossary

creative making something using your own ideas and how you feel inside

gallery place where art is displayed for people to look at

portrait picture of somebody

self-portrait picture that you draw of yourself

surface something that an artist draws on, such as paper

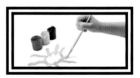

texture how a surface looks and feels

tools things you use to make art, such as pencils and crayons

Find Out More

Book

Thomas, Isabel. *Drawing (Action Art)*.
Chicago: Heinemann-Raintree, 2005.

Website

Find out about Van Gogh's drawings and try making marks
on this Website:
www.metmuseum.org/explore/van_gogh/menu.html

Index